MONTANA
where it all began...

by S. Archie

Copyright © 2025 by S. Archie
All rights reserved.

No part of this book may be reproduced, stored in a retrieval system, or transmitted in any form or by any means—electronic, mechanical, photocopying, recording, or otherwise—without the prior written permission of the author, except for brief quotations used in reviews or scholarly works.

This is a work of nonfiction. Some names and identifying details may have been changed to protect the privacy of individuals.

Cover Design: S. Archie

ISBN: 9798313023373

Printed in the United States of America

First Edition

"For I know the plans I have for you," declares the Lord, "plans to prosper you and not to harm you, plans to give you hope and a future."
—Jeremiah 29:11

TABLE OF CONTENTS

Introduction 1

Chapter 1: Snatched Up 3

Chapter 2: Torn Apart 7

Chapter 3: The Group Home 11

Chapter 4: Ride or Die 14

Chapter 5: Savage Mode 20

Chapter 6: The Run Out 25

Chapter 7: A Hard Lesson 30

Chapter 8: Trapped 36

Chapter 9: Chameleon Mode 40

Chapter 10: The Game 44

Chapter 11: The Set-Up 48

Chapter 12: The Hole 51

Chapter 13: New Territory 54

Chapter 14: The Switch Up 57

Chapter 15: The Chapel Hustle 61

Chapter 16: The Release 63

Chapter 17: Out the Gate 66

Chapter 18: All Gas, No Brakes 70

Chapter 19: Crash Season 74

Chapter 20: New Money, Same Me 80

Chapter 21: The Wait... 85

Author's Note 88

Introduction

Most of this shit is true. Some of it is or isn't. For legal and entertainment purposes, let's just say I'll leave it up to you to figure out what's real and what's been rearranged. This is not an autobiography. This is a raw, unfiltered look into my world and the things I may or may not have experienced. Some names have been changed. Some characters are real. Some are a mix of more than one person. But the energy, the pain, the choices, the grind—that's all me.

Not every story starts with sunshine and second chances. Some are born in the dark. And in those shadows, survival isn't promised. It's earned. The only way to make it out is to fight like hell through every scar, every lie, and every betrayal.

Montana is a story built on choices. Some reckless. Some desperate. Some made with nothing left but a dream and a heartbeat. It's a mirror held up to the system, to the streets, and to the trauma that shapes us when nobody teaches us better. In this world, survival and loyalty blur so much that you can't even tell the difference. This book is about the cost of learning life's hardest lessons too early and being expected to survive anyway.

This story follows a girl who became a woman without a fair shot. She grew up in chaos. Betrayal was normal. Struggle was daily. She adapted or got crushed. Every chapter takes you deeper into her world, where identity is tangled in trauma and freedom is a word most people just talk about. In this world, love comes with conditions, loyalty is bought, and pain is passed down like tradition.

But Montana isn't just about crime or consequence. It's about breaking and choosing to rebuild. It's about having nothing left but your name and your will. This story doesn't flinch. From jailhouse politics to the mental breakdowns nobody talks about, from love that hits like a drug to heartbreak that hits harder, it's all in here.

Through these pages, you'll walk with a woman who's been through hell and is still standing. Still pushing. Still figuring it out. She's not perfect. She's not polished. But she's real. She's a reflection of every woman who's ever been boxed in, counted out, and left to clean up a mess she didn't create.

This ain't just her story. It's the story of so many others. It's for the ones who got lost in the system. For the ones who still ain't found peace. For the ones who had to become hard just to survive. It's for the women with war behind their eyes and love still buried somewhere under all that pain.

This is for you.
This is for us.
Welcome to Montana.

Chapter 1: Snatched Up

Marcus's scream sliced through the silence like a knife. Not a whimper. Not a fuss. A full-blown, gut-wrenching cry that snatched me straight out of sleep. I shot up, heart pounding. It was past midnight. The apartment was still, too still. No keys jangling. No creak of the front door. Mama wasn't home. Again.

I didn't even bother turning on the light. Just moved through the dark like I'd done a hundred times before. His door was cracked. I pushed it open and found him sitting up in bed, hugging that beat-up teddy bear I won at that busted-ass carnival years ago. His face was soaked, eyes wide, trembling.

"I want Mama," he choked out, like the words alone might bring her back.

I sat beside him, pulling him close. "She'll be home soon," I whispered, knowing damn well that was a lie. I didn't know where the hell Mama was. Only thing I knew was it wasn't here.

Out in the living room, the TV played low with one of those late-night infomercials about miracle blenders or some bullshit. A bottle of gin sat tipped on the floor, the label peeling, half-empty like her promises. Same scene. Different night. Mama had been doing good for a while. Clocking in at Walmart, making dinner, even laughing at dumb jokes. But when that darkness crept back in, it swallowed her whole. And it took pieces of us with it.

Marcus eventually cried himself to sleep. I didn't. I laid on the couch, eyes glued to the front door, listening to every little sound. Sirens echoed in the distance, and something in my stomach twisted. That kind of twist you don't ignore.

Then headlights.

I jumped up, heartbeat loud in my ears. She stumbled toward the door, heels in one hand, purse dangling, hair wild like she'd been caught in a storm. I opened the door before she could even reach for her keys.

"Mama."

"Tasha?" Her voice slurred. "What you doin' up?"

I crossed my arms. "Where you been?"

She sighed, brushing past me like I was in her way. "Minding grown folks' business."

No apology. No explanation. Just the usual.

I should've let it slide. I should've just shut up. But Marcus's voice was still ringing in my head.

"He was cryin' for you," I said. "All night."

That made her pause. She didn't snap. Didn't yell. Just slumped down on the couch like all the fight left her body.

"I ain't mean to stay out so long, baby. I'm tryin'."

Trying. That word burned. Trying would've meant not pouring liquor for breakfast. Trying would've meant showing up when it mattered. But I bit my tongue, grabbed a blanket, and threw it over her shoulders.

"Yeah," I mumbled. "I know."

I did know. I knew she loved us in her own broken way. But love couldn't keep the lights on. Love couldn't tuck Marcus in at night. And love sure as hell couldn't save her from herself.

Then it happened. Three knocks. Loud. Heavy. Final.

I froze.

Opened the door just a crack and there they were. A woman in a stiff blazer with fake sympathy in her eyes, and a cop with his hand resting on his belt like we were already guilty.

"Good evening," she said, all sugar and lies. "I'm Ms. Whitaker from Child Protective Services. This is Officer Daniels. We need to speak with your mother."

CPS. My heart dropped into my shoes.

"She's sleepin'," I said, blocking the doorway.

Ms. Whitaker leaned in, peeking past me like I wasn't even there. "We got a call."

Officer Daniels spotted the bottle. That's all it took.

"I said we're fine," I snapped.

But fine didn't matter. Not to them.

In minutes, everything unraveled. Mama woke up, confused, pleading, clinging to us like her touch could reverse it.

"Please," she kept saying. "Don't take my babies."

But the begging didn't stop them. They took us anyway.

I held Marcus tight in the back of that car while Mama stood on the porch, barefoot, sobbing under the porch light. Her arms stretched out like she could pull us back from the other side of hell. Her voice cracked the night open.

Marcus shook in my arms, mumbling through tears. "I want Mama."

"I know," I whispered. My voice cracked too.

I pressed my hand against the glass, watching her collapse to her knees in the yard, broken in a way I'd never seen before.

And me?

I sat there, fourteen years old, holding my baby brother like I was his mother, his protector, his only damn lifeline.

I didn't have answers. I didn't have a plan.

But in that moment, I made myself a promise. No matter what it took. No matter how long it took. I'd get us back. I'd find a way to pull us out the system, out the chaos, out the pit they threw us in. I'd bring us home.

Chapter 2: Torn Apart

They didn't even give us a chance to say goodbye. The moment CPS stepped in, they tore me and Marcus apart like we were just paperwork. Names on a file. Not a brother and sister who had been each other's whole world since day one. They said I was too old to be placed with him. That was it. No compassion. No second thought. Just a decision that ripped the only piece of home I had left out of my hands.

I begged them not to separate us. I cried. I screamed. I ran after the car they stuffed him into like it would make a difference. But it didn't. They tossed me into another vehicle like I was a stray they didn't know what to do with. One minute he was there, holding my hand. The next, he was gone.

The first night without him broke something in me.

I kept waking up in a cold, unfamiliar bed, expecting to hear his voice. To feel the tug of his little fingers on my arm. I could still hear his sniffles in the dark, still remember the way he curled up beside me when he was scared. I had spent years protecting him. When Mama disappeared, I made sure he ate. When he cried, I told stories to help him fall asleep. When life came at us hard, I stood in front of him and took the hit. And now I was just alone.

Not just alone in foster care. Alone in the world.

They stuck me in an emergency placement home. A crowded house with too many kids, not enough food, and even less love. The foster parents tried to act like everything was normal. They offered snacks and told jokes. But they weren't mine. They weren't Marcus. They weren't Mama.

And Mama? I hated her for putting us in this situation. I missed her too. I wanted her to show up, to fight for us, to fix what she broke. Even though I knew she wouldn't. She always said this time would be different. She held us tight and promised she wouldn't let go. Then let us fall the moment temptation knocked.

I was only fourteen, but I had already lived through more than most adults. I had taken care of myself for years. I had taken care of Marcus. Hell, some days I had taken care of Mama. I had kept things together long before CPS came in and ripped them apart. And now, nobody cared. Not the caseworker who barely looked me in the eye. Not the foster mom who was too tired to ask how I was doing. Not the other kids, who were all too busy drowning in their own mess to notice mine.

I stopped talking. I stopped eating. I was trapped in a kind of silence that didn't scream. It just sat on my chest, heavy and thick, making it hard to breathe. Nobody asked if I was okay. Maybe they already knew the answer. Or maybe they just didn't give a damn.

Then came the move. Another placement. Another stranger's house. Another round of questions I didn't want to answer. I didn't ask where we were going. I didn't care. Nothing mattered.

But when the car stopped in front of that building, I knew this was different. This wasn't a house. It wasn't even a home. It was a facility. Big. Cold. Empty in the way places get when people come and go without ever belonging.

I walked in with my arms crossed tight over my chest, trying to disappear into myself. The air smelled like bleach and something old. The walls were pale and dull, covered in motivational posters that felt like lies. A woman with tired eyes and a stiff smile greeted me at the door.

"Welcome, Natasha," she said like she was giving me a prize instead of a sentence. "We're going to take great care of you here."

I didn't believe her.

Behind her, a group of girls stood whispering near the hallway. One of them laughed. The tall one with the braids. I recognized the look in her eyes. Territorial. Curious. Dangerous. I kept my face still and walked past them like I didn't see a thing.

The woman led me past a common room where girls lounged on old couches, staring at a small TV. No one said a word. No one smiled. She stopped in front of a long room with twin beds lined up like a shelter. No curtains. No privacy. Just a row of mattresses, blue vinyl covers, and chipped plastic dressers.

"This will be your space," she said, pointing at the bed in the corner.

The blanket was thin. The pillow looked like it had been through war. And all around me, girls watched from their beds, braiding hair, writing in journals, or just staring. I could already tell who ran this place and who stayed quiet to survive.

"This is home for now," the woman added, patting my shoulder like she meant it.

Home. The word hit me like a punch. This wasn't home. Home was gone the second they took Marcus.

I sat on the edge of the bed, fists clenched in my lap, spine straight like I was bracing for impact. The second she walked out, the whispering turned real.

"She looks scared."

I didn't flinch. I didn't blink. I stared straight ahead, blank-faced. I knew the game. In places like this, weakness was bait. Blood in the water.

I wasn't about to bleed for them.

So, I did what I'd always done. I built another wall. Taller. Stronger. Because if nobody was going to protect me, I'd protect myself.

I didn't know how long I'd be here. Didn't know what kind of pain was waiting behind those walls. But I knew one thing.

Whatever it took, I would survive.

I always did.

Chapter 3: The Group Home

The first night in the group home, I didn't sleep. Not because I wasn't tired, I was, but because I refused to close my eyes around a bunch of strangers. You learn really quick in places like that: never let your guard down.

The place was an old, three-story building that used to be an office or something. Now it was a holding tank for kids that nobody wanted. The walls were dull beige, the beds were stiff cots with thin sheets, and the smell of bleach barely covered the scent of sweat, piss, and despair. The halls echoed with doors slamming, girls yelling, and the "staff" barking orders like we were in boot camp.

"Lights out!" they shouted that first night. I just lay there, staring up at the ceiling, listening to the sounds of girls whispering, plotting, and fighting sleep like I was. It was my first time being around so many different people. I was used to being home alone with Marcus and Mama whenever she would be home. Now, I had to figure out how to move in a place full of strangers. Who was cool? Who was dangerous? Who could be trusted?

From the minute I walked in, I could feel the eyes on me. Sizing me up. I wasn't the smallest girl in there, but I wasn't the biggest either. I had two options: become the prey or become the problem. I chose the latter. Girls in here didn't fight with fists first; they fought with words, with rumors, with humiliation. You didn't just have to be tough; you had to be unshakable. I learned that really quick.

"Look at the new girl."

"She thinks she cute."

"Bet her mama's a crackhead."

The first week, it was just talk. Little jokes, little tests. I ignored it. Stayed quiet. Watched. Learned. But in a place like this, silence ain't strength. Silence is weakness. I never let them see me cry. Not once. Not even when I lay awake at night, staring at the ceiling, feeling more alone than I ever had in my life. I missed Marcus. I missed my mama, even after everything. I missed normal. But missing people didn't change nothing. Some nights were worse than others. Some nights, I'd press my face into the pillow and wish I could disappear. Some nights, I actually did.

One of the staff was a man. He wasn't supposed to be in our rooms after dark, but rules didn't matter to him. Power did. It started small. His hand resting on my shoulder just a second too long. A stare that clung to my body like smoke. A joke laced with something I couldn't name but knew was wrong. Then one night, he pressed himself against me as I passed him in the hallway. His breath was sour, close to my ear. "You're growing up real nice," he whispered. His hand slid lower than it ever should have.

I froze. My stomach turned. I wanted to run, to scream, to slap the smirk off his face. But I didn't. I knew how this worked. If you fight back, you're the problem. If you tell, nobody believes you.

So I did what I'd learned to do best. I survived.

But surviving came with a cost. What happened that night didn't end that night. It became a routine. Twice a week, like clockwork, he would pull me from my living quarters. He would violate my body and strip away what little innocence I had left. I stopped being a child and became something else entirely. My body didn't feel like mine anymore. Every time I looked at myself, I felt dirty. Every time someone else looked at me, I felt shame.

He was the only one who was nice to me. That's what made it even worse. I had to be nicer to him. That's how it worked. His kindness was a trap, a leash wrapped in fake comfort and poison. Over time, I started to feel things in my body I didn't understand. Cravings that confused me. I began to associate touch with attention, pain with value. The only affection I ever knew came from manipulation. The only comfort came with a cost.

I avoided him when I could. I timed my steps, tracked his schedule, tried to disappear. But he always found a way. A hand against my back. A whisper when no one was watching. His eyes crawling over me from across the room. I stopped sleeping. I stopped smiling. The bullying, the fights, the violence. They bounced off me like nothing. Because inside, I had already disappeared. I wasn't scared anymore. I wasn't angry. I wasn't anything.

No escape. Just time.

I spent months in that place, counting the days, pretending like none of it touched me. But it did. It touched every part of me. At night, I'd lay on that thin mattress and think about Marcus. Was he okay? Did he still remember me? I thought about Mama and whether she was still vanishing into the night or if maybe she had finally figured it out. I thought about the girl I used to be before the world carved her into this hollow thing.

But thinking too much gets you hurt, so I stopped.

I became what they needed me to be. Cold. Tough. Untouchable. Because in that place, the only way to make it through was to kill the part of you that still cared. And I did. Piece by piece, I buried her.

Chapter 4: Ride or Die

By the time I hit sixteen, life had already hardened me in ways I never saw coming. Bouncing between group homes, foster houses, and strangers' couches, I learned that nothing was permanent and the only person I could trust was myself. Eventually, I said fuck the system.

Technically, I wasn't emancipated. I just ran off from my last group home, and nobody looked too hard. I slept wherever I could, ate whatever I found, and did what I had to do to stay alive.

School? I went off and on, mostly just for the free lunch. Some stubborn piece of me still refused to let go completely. But the truth was, I was living on the edge. Alone. Always alone.

Then, shortly after my seventeenth birthday, I met Nasir.

He was nineteen, with a mouth full of gold teeth and a car that rumbled whenever his foot touched the gas pedal. Fast mouth. Faster ride. I first saw him outside the corner store, leaning against his candy-painted Chevy, flirting with some girl. He caught me looking as I came out with a soda and a bag of chips, my dinner for the night.

"Aye, Red. You got a name?" I rolled my eyes and kept walking. He followed anyway, persistent and bold. There was something about his cockiness that I liked. The way he smiled while pursuing me, like he already knew how the story would end. Before I knew it, I was laughing with him in that parking lot for hours and for once I felt comfortable.

That was the beginning.

Nasir became my escape. With him, I wasn't a runaway. I wasn't a statistic. I was just his girl. He took me on late-night drives, music loud, city lights flying past like dreams I never thought I'd touch. He taught me how to drive stick in that old Chevy, his hands guiding mine slow and firm over the gears.

After two months of being together every day, he handed me keys to a beat-up Honda he got from some auction. I didn't ask where the money came from. I didn't care. Nobody had ever given me anything before. But Nasir did. And with him, I finally felt like I belonged.

He introduced me to his people. Not family, but they acted like it. A circle of guys he got money with. They threw parties at recreation centers every weekend, charging ten bucks at the door and making good money. I got in on the hustle, too, I was in charge of getting the women to show up. We were making money, but once we split it four ways, we'd all be broke again soon.

His hustle was consistent, he did whatever he had to do to keep money in his pockets. This nigga was a flat out thief. He stole phones, did home invasions, he even was into shoplifting. He never paid for anything out of stores, and neither did I. I knew it was wrong, but I had gone my whole life with nothing. Now, I had something, and I wasn't about to let go.

Then there was the way he touched me.

Nasir didn't rush anything. He made love to every part of my body slowly, like he had all night. His hands memorized me. His lips spoke in silence across my skin. There was no pain, no confusion, no pressure. Just warmth. Just want. He looked at me like I was precious, not broken. And for the first time, I didn't feel like just a body or just a burden. I felt seen. He had me craving more of him. Not just the sex, but the comfort, the closeness. I had never known love, not like that. But I felt it with Nasir. And I was already falling, deep.

So when he asked me for something, I didn't hesitate.

One hot summer night, we were parked in my Honda listening to slow jams. He was quiet. Real quiet. Then he put out his joint and turned toward me.

"I need you for something, Tasha."

I sat up. My chest already tight. "Wassup?"

He looked me in the eyes. "We're about to hit the Pizza Hut up on Sunset Strip after they close. It's an easy lick."

A break-in. My heart dropped. Does this nigga want me to ski up and run in a pizza joint with a pistol?

I should've said no, hell, I wanted to. But Nasir's eyes were locked on mine, full of that same hunger and trust I had grown addicted to. I owed him. He had given me a place, a car, a home. And love. Real love. Or what I thought was love.

I nodded. "I got you."

Didn't even ask what he needed. Just said yes. Dumb. Stupid. And lost.

The night of the lick, I found out that I would only be needed as the driver. They tried to make it seem as if it was an easy task, but in my mind, it was the hardest. Because if I fucked up, we'd all go to jail. I was nervous as hell. My hands shook as I gripped the wheel with the engine running.

We loaded up in my Honda, everyone dressed in all black. I pulled at the stop sign near the pizza joint and turned my lights off as Nasir, Rico, and Jamal ran across the street and slipped through the back door. I stayed on lookout.

Three minutes passed. THREE. Then flashing red lights.

Already?

I wanted to leave. My body told me to drive, but I couldn't. I wasn't leaving Nasir. My man. My comfort. My ride-or-die.

They all came running out, Nasir holding a large duffel bag. "GO! GO!" Nasir yelled.

I slammed the gas. Tires screeched. The alley blurred. In the mirror, a security guard screamed into a radio. Then came the sirens. Red and blue closing in on us, fast.

"Shit! Drive faster!" Jamal screamed.

"You got this, bae," Nasir said from the passenger seat, trying to keep me calm.

I sped through a red light and almost clipped a car. No good. We weren't getting away.

"Turn!" Nasir yelled. I did.

Dead end.

"No time! Everybody out!"

We ran. Through alleys. Over fences. The police were close. I could hear them, it was almost as if I could feel them. The hairs on l arms began to stand up, and although I was full on in the middle of a high speed chase, everything felt as if it were in slow motion and about to come to an end.

Then we hit a tall chain-link fence. Rico and Jamal were gone. Nasir jumped first, smooth like he'd done it a hundred times. I grabbed the fence.

"FREEZE!"

A flashlight beam hit me.

Nasir dropped on the other side. He was safe. He turned to me.

"Nasir! Help me!" I reached out.

For a second, he hesitated. Then he backed up.

"I'm sorry, bae. I'll get you out."

Then he ran.

He left me.

This nigga really left me.

"Come down now!" the officer yelled, gun drawn.

I climbed down, rage boiling in my chest. They slammed me against the wall, cuffed me like I was the only one who mattered.

"Dumb ass girl out here playin' getaway driver and the only one who ain't get away," the officer said.

I didn't even hear the rest. The only thing replaying in my mind was how my man, my protector, my partner, had left me.

I gave him everything. Well, at least I thought I did. I did everything for him, even catered to is friends. I kept everything together at the apartment. I counted the money after every lick and not once had I ever even thought about deceiving or betraying him. And when it mattered most, he gave me nothing.

The backseat of the police car smelled like sweat and ass. I sat there, face frowned up and sitting uncomfortable as my hands were tied behind my back. I had been ride-or-die. I was ready to go to war behind that man. But when it was time to ride for me?

He had hauled ass.

The pain was deep, but it came with clarity. I bit my lip until it bled. I wouldn't cry. I wouldn't fold. I had survived worse.

This was just another lesson.

Ride or die?

I was done with that.

From now on, the only person I was riding for was me.

Chapter 5: Savage Mode

They booked me for burglary and assault. The assault charge came because one of Nasir's dumbass friends knocked over the security guard on the way out. The cops tried to press me for names, but I wasn't saying shit. I wasn't a snitch. And after what Nasir did, I wasn't trusting nobody, definitely not the police. So, in the end, it was just me.

Because I was seventeen, they sent me to juvie while my case worked its way through court. Juvie was its own kind of hell. A few of the girls tried to play tough by sizing me up, but I gave them the same looks they gave me. I wasn't easily intimidated so they usually picked on the smaller juvies, or the white ones. I'd been through worse. At least here, I knew where I stood. Nobody was my friend. Nobody was my family. If someone pushed, I pushed back. If someone hit, I hit harder. It was simple, I'd had enough of people taking advantage of me, and I started defending myself long before entering this hell hole.

I really didn't trust anyone and didn't want to be around anyone. One day during leisure time, I stuck my middle finger up at the officer in the control room because his creepy ass was always watching me. That alone was enough to get me sent to the hole, and I was fine with that. Every time the disciplinary board would come around for my hearing, I'd refuse; because of that I wasn't released from confinement.

After seventy-five days of being locked up, I finally saw a judge. Since it was my first big charge, they tried me as a youthful offender instead of an adult.

That saved my ass. I ended up with time served, probation, and a record that was gonna follow me forever. But I walked out of that courthouse free.

And who the hell do I see waiting on the steps? Nasir. He had the nerve to show up. Leaning against a pole, both hands in his pockets, looking at me like he was glad to see me. Like he hadn't left me that night. Like he didn't run. He still was fine as hell too. Golds were glistening, dimples showing, eyes staring into my soul. Part of me wanted to hug him. Part of me wanted to punch him in the face.

I walked up slow. We locked eyes.

"Tasha," he started, scratching his neck like a crackhead. "I panicked. I thought you'd get over the fence."

"Save it." My voice was cold. I wasn't the same girl he left behind.

"You left me, Nasir. You let me take the fall while you ran like a little bitch. Ride or die, huh?"

His face crumbled. "I know. I messed up. I was scared."

He reached for my waist, but I stepped back so fast it made him flinch.

"I missed you," he kept going, voice low. "I tried to check on you. Soon as I heard you were getting out; I had to come."

I should've walked away. Right then. I should've told him to go to hell. But looking at him, I hated him, and I loved him all at once. That's what made me dangerous. I was too soft for everyone else. And too hard for myself.

I kept walking. He followed.

"Montana, please," he begged.

I stopped. Turned.

"Montana?"

He nodded. "Yeah. Montana. Bold. Bossy. Badass. That's you."

I smirked. That name? I liked that name. Tasha was gone. Montana was here to stay.

He took a step closer, dropping his voice.

"You ain't snitch," he whispered. "That means something. You are definitely my ride or die and I'm not letting you go. I'm sorry. I swear."

I knew he was lying. I could see it in his weak-ass eyes. But I let him trail behind me anyway. That night, I was back in his bed, stretched out and getting my back blown out. Just like that. Toxic. Co-dependent. Messy as hell. But I wasn't ready to be alone, I'd had enough of that.

For a few weeks, things were chill. I kept my head low. Checked in with my PO. Worked some bullshit dishwashing job at the Subway near by. Nasir even toned it down for me. We played house like we were normal. Like we weren't both turned on by living the fast life. This new straight and narrow life had become boring as hell, and I was craving for some action.

We finally agreed to have a gathering at the apartment and charge at the door for some fast cash. I recognized some faces. Rico. A couple of his day-one, the niggas that jumped out and left me were in attendance too. Then there were new faces. One of them? Some female, all up on Nasir. I watched them from across the room, sipping my drink. The first time she touched his arm, I let it slide. The second time, I clenched my jaw. The third time?

I snatched her ass up. My fingers were in her hair before I even thought about it.

"Back the fuck up," I growled.

She screamed, grabbing at my hands. People jumped up. Nasir yanked me back.

"Montana! Chill!"

Nah. Fuck that. I wasn't some random bitch. I wasn't replaceable. She ran out, calling me crazy. I didn't give a damn.

Nasir tried to calm me down. I wasn't hearing it.

"You make me look stupid again, and I swear to God…" I didn't finish. Didn't have to. He knew. And I stormed out.

I walked the streets for hours. No tears. No fear. Just rage. And that's when it clicked. I wasn't just mad at him. I was mad at everything. Mama. Marcus. The system. The whole damn world. I was done. No more playing nice. No more holding back.

Eventually, I cooled off and went back to Nasir's place.

He must've thought that I wasn't coming back. Where the hell else did I have to go? He knew that I didn't have anyone else to turn to.

I opened the door, walked inside like I lived there because I basically did, and there he was. Laid up in bed with that same bitch. The same one whose head I almost knocked off her shoulders at the party. Her hair was all over his chest. He looked up like he had just seen a ghost.

I blacked out.

I beat his ass. I beat her ass. I beat both their asses. Again. No warning. No words. Just hands. I dragged her out the bed and onto the floor. She screamed, tried to fight back, but I was already on ten. Nasir tried to pull me off, but I wasn't letting up. Not this time.

When it was over, I was standing in the middle of the room, chest heaving, fists balled. They both looked shook. And I? I was just done.

But I didn't leave. I made sure to see miss thing out, I slammed the door so hard behind her that the front room window shattered. He and I argued more throughout the night, and he fed me some bullshit ass story that she was just something to do while I was away.

While I was away, serving time for a crime that he and his friends had committed. The audacity of him to need someone else to lean on while I was left all alone.

I had nowhere else to go.

I stayed. I started stacking money, watching everything, planning my getaway in silence.

Chapter 6: The Run Out

After all the bullshit with Nasir's no-good ass, I started being there less and less. I couldn't stand the sight of him. I wouldn't even sleep in the bed at the apartment. At that point, we were basically roommates. No love. No warmth. Just silence and avoidance. I'd come in late, eat something, crash on the couch, and keep my distance. It wasn't even about being mad anymore. I just didn't feel anything for him. I didn't want to be touched, didn't want to be looked at. And when I did look at him, all I saw was a liar who left me behind and thought a few gifts could fix it.

I felt like a stranger in a place I once called home. But I stayed, because I didn't have anywhere else to go, yet. I was biding my time, stacking what little I could, and figuring out my next move. I knew I couldn't stay there forever. I could feel the walls closing in every time I walked through that door.

Every now an then I would chill at the park killing time with a couple of girls I knew from the neighborhood. Keisha and Shay. They weren't my real friends, but I wasn't looking for friendship. They were wild, slick mouthed, and tired of life's bullshit, just like me. Keisha was a deep brown complexion with high cheekbones, thick lashes, and the kind of confidence that could shut a room down. Shay was slim with glowing caramel skin and big eyes that gave her a reason to be nosey as hell. Her hair was full of natural curls, pulled back into a puff that bounced when she laughed. I considered them as my homegirls, we always had a ball when in each other's company.

We were sitting under the gazebo, sipping Grey Goose from the bottle and telling stories about who had the worst childhood. Keisha talked about bouncing between different family members. Shay talked about how her dad was in prison and her mom didn't even know what school she went to. Me, I just stayed quiet, I'd been through too much to even want to think about it, let alone talk. I actually had never told anyone about the things I'd lived through.

As the liquor started to settle in, Shay nudged me. "Aye, Montana, you still got that Honda?"

I shrugged. "Yeah. Why?"

The Honda had somehow survived my arrest. Nasir had picked it up and handed it back like it was supposed to mean something. One of his weak attempts to make it right.

Keisha grinned, twirling a strand of her hair. "We got an idea. Something quick. You down for a thrill?"

I squinted at her. "What kind of thrill?"

Shay leaned in like she was about to tell me a secret. "Ever done a run out?"

I laughed. "A run out? Like a snatch and grab?"

They both nodded like it was the best idea in the world.

"What, y'all trying to steal some lip gloss and candy bars?" I asked.

Keisha sucked her teeth. "Nah. We're talking about that new boutique on Commercial. Designer shit. Bags. Clothes. Real money. They only got one security guard and he's slow as hell. We walk in, grab what we want, and bounce. In and out."

It was actually stupid as fuck.

But I was reckless, angry, and tired of being broke. I didn't even blink.

"Alright," I said, smirking. "Let's do it."

We piled into my Honda, still tipsy, still hyped. Shay would drive since I didn't have as much luck being a getaway driver. Me and Keisha would grab the items. We tossed the bottle in the back, turned up the music, and began to let our adrenaline build up.

When we got to the boutique, we split up like we were shopping for real. I browsed racks, my heart pounding. Keisha walked toward the bags. The security guard was half-asleep near the door, sitting on a stool with his eyes barely open. Too easy.

Keisha held up a purse and shouted across the store, "T, look at this one!"

I had already told her not to call me by name once we entered the store.

I walked over, playing along. "Girl, I love this."

Then she grabbed another bag and ran towards the door.

That was the signal.

I snatched a few more off the rack and ran behind her, grabbing a few pair of sunglasses as I ran out of the door. Sunglasses in one hand, designer bags in the other. The guard stood up, confused, yelling for us to stop. But Shay already had the car pulled up at the curb, doors open.

We dove in, Keisha laughing so hard she could barely breathe. "Go, go, go!"

Shay must've pressed the gas pedal to the floor because the tires screeched. The guard chased us, but he didn't stand a chance. I could barely breathe. Between the vodka and the thrill, my chest was burning. I looked down at the bags in my lap and couldn't help it. I laughed too.

It felt like one of those scenes from a movie. I felt alive.

We didn't stop until we pulled behind an old warehouse. Empty lot. No eyes. We jumped out and dumped the bags on the concrete. Gucci. Louis. Dolce. Michael Kors. Keisha picked up a pair of sunglasses and posed in them. Shay clutched a purse like it was already hers.

"This Never-full is mine," I said, holding up the Louis. "Y'all can split the rest since it's my car."

They sucked their teeth but didn't argue.

That's when it hit me. The fun faded just enough for that tight feeling to creep into my gut. What if somebody caught my license plate? What if they got caught and turned on me? I had to get from around them, I began to think about the last incident and immediately started feeling weird inside.

I dropped them off quick and headed to Nasir's.

By the time I got back to Nasir's apartment, the sun was setting. He wasn't there, and that was fine with me. I needed space. I laid out the bags on the couch and tried them on in the mirror, one by one. I wanted to feel proud. Wanted to feel like somebody. But all I felt was numb.

Later that night, Keisha texted me.

"Yo that was fun. Next time we hit an even bigger lick."

I stared at the message, then locked my phone without replying. My gut felt tight again, that same pressure like time was running out.

Every dumb thing I did, every reckless moment, every time I didn't get caught, it was all adding up.

I didn't know when, but I knew. One day, the clock was gonna hit zero.

And when it did, there would be no running.

Chapter 7: A Hard Lesson

It turned out my instincts were dead right. The karma from that run out didn't happen immediately. In fact, a couple of weeks passed, and I almost forgot about it. But consequences have a way of catching up, especially when you're already on the system's radar. It was early one morning when the reckoning came. I was crashing at Nasir's still, though our relationship had become even more distant. He was out late most nights and so was I, and not together either. Trust between us was thin, but toxicity kept us together, for now.

I remember waking up to the sound of pounding on the apartment door. For a split second, I thought it was Nasir coming back drunk and forgetting his keys. But then I heard voices on the other side of the door, and when I listened a little closer, I heard a walkie talkie. "Police! Open up!" a man shouted. My heart dropped. There was only one reason the police would be banging on our door early in the morning, they wanted me. Maybe Nasir too, but definitely me.

I was too afraid. I stood there covering my mouth and hopping around on my toes in one spot, trying to figure out how I could get out of there without them seeing me. The pounding grew louder, the whole door rattling. "We have a warrant! Open the door now or we'll break it down!" I heard. My mind raced, thinking of the stolen items I still had stashed in the closet, the purses and some electronics that Nasir had recently stolen. Too late to hide anything now.

I considered not opening the door, but I knew that would just make things worse. Taking a deep breath, I stepped forward and cracked it open, trying to appear half asleep and confused. In an instant, the door was shoved all the way open. Half a dozen officers stormed in, guns out. "Hands up!" one screamed at me. I raised my hands, heart hammering. They swarmed the small apartment. Two officers pushed me against the wall and snapped cuffs on my wrists before I could blink. Others fanned out, flipping over the couch, dumping out drawers. It was chaos. I didn't even bother protesting or asking what this was about. I knew. They had either linked me to the run out or my PO had violated me for skipping appointments, or both.

One female officer read me my rights while another watched, her expression unreadable. "...for burglary and grand larceny, and violation of probation," she recited. Yep. There it was. Burglary and grand larceny, that had to be the boutique. And I was screwed on the probation end too. I slumped against the wall as they finished searching the place. They found the stolen purses, a pair of sunglasses, along with a few phones Nasir had stashed. It was more than enough evidence. When they led me out of the apartment, I saw a couple of our nosy neighbors peeking from their doorways. I kept my head high and my face blank, even as shame crawled up my spine. I was being paraded out like some trophy catch, and damned if I'd give anyone the satisfaction of seeing me cry.

Downstairs, they guided me into the back of a squad car. As the door closed, I caught sight of a familiar face at the corner of the building, Keisha. She was half-hidden behind a fence, eyes wide as saucers. Our eyes locked for a brief moment. Then she turned and ran. Oh, did this feel familiar. So much for being partners in crime. In the end, when faced with real trouble, they looked out for number one. I wasn't surprised. Disappointed, maybe, but not surprised. I'd known better than to trust them deeply. Still, a bitter taste filled my mouth as the cruiser pulled away.

The ride to the station was quiet. I stared at the cage separating me from the officers in the front seat and let reality sink in. I was in deep now. I had violated probation and picked up new felony charges while already having one strike. The system was not going to be lenient this time. I was looking at serious time, and that thought should have terrified me. Oddly, it didn't. It was almost a relief, in a way, to have the inevitable finally happen. I'd been living recklessly, and I knew it. Now it was time to face the music.

At the precinct, they processed me, fingerprints, mugshot, the whole routine I'd been through before. A detective tried to talk to me about the boutique theft, offering me leniency if I named my accomplices. I responded to him with a cold stare and said nothing. I wasn't about to play their game. Keisha and Shay hadn't gotten caught, and I definitely wasn't helping the police do their job. I was done talking. Whatever was coming, I'd face it on my own.

Later, sitting alone in a holding cell, I had plenty of time to think. The adrenaline had faded, leaving me exhausted. For the first time in a long while, I let myself slump and feel the weight of it all. Seventeen years old, and here I was, headed to jail for real this time. Not just a juvie bid, actual time. A hard lesson indeed, I thought bitterly. All my life I'd been failed by people, by Mama, by the system, by Nasir, by fake friends, and now I'd failed myself. The common thread in all of it was me. Every time I hoped or trusted, I got burned. Every time I lashed out and broke the rules, I made things worse. It was like I was trapped in a cycle I couldn't escape, hurt, rebel, hurt worse.

I pressed my back against the cool cement wall of the cell and closed my eyes. No tears came. I felt empty, beyond tears. Maybe this was where I was always going to end up, I chuckled. Maybe some people just don't get happy endings. The thought made me angry, but I was too drained to hold onto that anger. Instead, I pictured Marcus's face, trying to remember the last time I'd seen my little brother. It had been years. Was he happy? Did he even remember me? Would he hear about what happened to his big sister? Part of me hoped not. I didn't want him to see what I had become.

As I sat there in the dim silence, I promised myself one thing, no more trusting anyone, including myself. Expect nothing, and you can't be disappointed. It was a horrible mindset, but it was all I had left to shield myself from the pain. I numbed myself to the fate that awaited me, convincing myself I didn't care. But deep down, a small voice, one I tried to smother, whispered that I did care. That I was terrified. Because I knew the hardest part was yet to come, and I would have to survive it alone.

Six months in county jail felt longer than any other time I had ever served, and its time is the hardest time to complete. Ain't no moving around, no real routine, no yard to stretch your legs in like prison. Just four walls, a filthy-ass mattress, and the constant reminder that you ain't got no control over your life.

The jail sat right in the heart of the city, but you wouldn't know it. It was tucked down some dirt road, surrounded by empty manufacturing buildings, like they wanted to make sure we were forgotten. The windows were tall, thin rectangles, just big enough for one person to peek out at a time, if you were lucky. Most of the time, all you'd see were the officers coming and going, looking through us like we were nothing. If you had visitors, you might catch a glimpse of them walking by, but even that wasn't comforting. Who the hell wants to talk through a filthy telephone, used by thousands of inmates, just to stare at your people through a thick, bulletproof glass?

That glass was a reminder. You ain't free. You belong to them. The whole place was designed to break you. Beds, if that's what you wanna call them, had to be made by 7 a.m. sharp. No exceptions. And once that sun went down, you better not even think about laying under that scratchy, thin ass blanket they gave you. I don't know why it mattered so much to them, but county jail ain't about comfort. It's about control. And if this was how my local jail was running things, I just knew prison was gonna be worse.

I did what I always did in a new spot, stayed quiet, observed, figured out who was who. But let's be real, no matter where I went, I was HER. My bunkie was Ash, and she was solid. Clean, cool, kept to herself. We clicked immediately. Our birthdays were a day apart, so we had that in common. That might not mean much on the outside, but inside, finding someone you actually vibe with is rare.

Most days, we'd sit out in rec, soaking up that little bit of sunlight we could get. But rec yard was a joke. It wasn't no real yard, just a basketball court surrounded by 20-foot concrete walls. No trees, no grass, just hard-ass cement and a tiny patch of sky teasing us from above. No benches, no chairs, nowhere to sit but the damn ground. So that's what we did, sat on the floor like we were hanging out on the block, talking about anything but jail. That was the closest we got to the outside world, unless we were chained together like slaves, getting transported to court to hear whatever fate the system had decided for us

Commissary? Trash. You could spend $40 a week, but what was there to buy? Chips, soups, and hot sausages. That's it. If you ain't have people sending you money, you were stuck eating that nasty-ass tray food. But I always found a way to make things work. I made friends with a nightshift officer. She was cool, one of the only ones who acted like she actually had a heart. She'd let me clean for her during her shift while we talked about life outside. And when nobody was watching, she'd bring me food from the outside.

I never told nobody. Not even Ash. Not because I didn't trust her, but because I didn't trust nobody in there. People smile in your face and snitch on you the second it benefits them. I wasn't about to lose my little bit of comfort over some jealous inmate running her mouth. That was county life, survive however you could. And if this was just jail, I could only imagine what prison had waiting for me.

Chapter 8: Trapped

I spent the next several months in county, awaiting my court date. At seventeen, I was technically still a minor, but with the severity of my charges and my previous record, they decided to charge me as an adult this time. I was still out on bond for the earlier burglary and assault charges when my court date finally arrived for all my offenses. They shuffled me into the courthouse in a blue jumpsuit and shackles, surrounded by guards. It was a far cry from the last time I'd walked into that building as a free girl. The memory of leaving court and seeing Nasir waiting felt like a joke in that moment. He wasn't here today. Nobody was.

The courtroom felt large and empty. As I was led to the defense table, I scanned the seats, mostly empty, saved for a few nosey spectators. I did notice a middle-aged woman with stress written all over her face, probably someone else's mom. No familiar faces. Mama wasn't there. I hadn't seen or heard from her in years; for all I knew, she might not even know I was locked up. Nasir certainly wasn't there; I doubted he even kept track of what happened after my arrest.

My public defender, a state-appointed, paperwork-pushing lady who barely remembered my name half the time, shuffled through a stack of papers trying to find my plea deal. She had advised me to take the deal, informing me that it was a one time offer, so I did. Guilty on all counts in exchange for a slightly reduced sentence. I didn't have the fight in me to go to trial anyway, plus I was practically homeless so prison would be my new free room and board. I just wanted to get it over with. The judge, an old white man sat in his wheelchair with a straight face and read out my charges and the agreed-upon sentencing terms. His voice was firm, not a bit of sympathy as he verbalized my charges, burglary, grand larceny, probation violation, assault as an accomplice. Hearing it all laid out like that, I felt strangely dissociated, like he was talking about someone else. The girl who did all that sounded like a lost cause, a menace to society. Maybe I was.

When he asked if I had anything to say before sentencing, I stood there and shook my head. What could I say? Sorry? I'd said that enough in my life, and it never fixed anything. So, I stayed silent. The sentence came swift and heavy, three years in state prison, with the possibility of work release in one and a half for good behavior. Three years. It could have been worse, I suppose, but it still hit me like a punch to the gut. At my age, three years felt like a lifetime. I'd be twenty by the time I got out, if I was lucky. An adult. Not that I ever really got to be a kid.

The gavel fell and that was it. The judge moved on to the next case, and I was escorted out. In the span of fifteen minutes, my fate was sealed. I was officially a convicted felon, heading to state prison. Oddly, I didn't feel the urge to cry or scream. I felt… relieved. This was just the next chapter of the same tragic story, wasn't it? The system had caught me in its teeth and wasn't letting go this time.

Back in my cell that night, the weight of it settled on me. I lay on the hard mat staring at the ceiling. Three years. I counted it out in my head, picturing a calendar. Three birthdays. Three Christmases. Marcus would be, what, almost fifteen when I got out? Would he even remember me by then? Did I want him to?

I felt trapped in more ways than one. Trapped physically behind bars and barbed wire that I'd soon be shipped off to. Trapped by my own mistakes that had led me here. Trapped in a life that seemed hell-bent on breaking me. It was a suffocating realization. I rolled onto my side, curling up as if I could hide from it all.

In the weeks that followed, as I awaited transfer to the state facility, I kept to myself. Fights broke out in the jail pods, newcomers cycled in and out, but I was in a holding pattern. Each night I would disappear into my own mind, the only place where I had any freedom left. I'd replay memories like old movies, Mama fixing us dinner, Marcus laughing as I pushed him on a swing, even Nasir's smile showing his golden teeth. These ghosts of my past were all I had for company.

I didn't have hope, literally, none. Hope felt too dangerous to hold onto, it could be snatched away too easily. But I did have a kind of grim resolve. I would do my time. I would keep my head down and survive prison, just as I had survived everything else. One day I would get out, and then… well, I'd figure that out if I lived to see it.

On the morning of my transfer, they shackled me once more and loaded me onto a bus with a dozen of other women. We were headed south to the female prison reception center, a place I'd only heard about in whispers from other inmates. As the bus rumbled down the highway, I stared out the window at the world I was leaving behind, streets, cars, people going to work or school. Regular life, the kind I'd never really had. My reflection in the glass looked back at me, a tough on the exterior young black woman who'd been through war and was heading off to the next battle.

"I'm not dead yet," I whispered to myself, so softly no one else could hear. It was something to hold onto. An affirmation. As long as I was alive, there was a chance, maybe not for happiness, not for some fairytale ending, but a chance to at least shape what came next. Even trapped in the system, my story was still mine, and it wasn't over.

It was a small spark of determination in the darkness, but for now, it was all I had. I closed my eyes and let that spark burn quietly inside me as the bus carried me off to a place that I didn't know what to expect.

Chapter 9: Chameleon Mode

I arrived at the state prison with my head high and my heart steady. I wasn't walking in like some broken girl crushed by the weight of my sentence, I was walking in like someone who had been here before, even if I technically hadn't. The thing about me? I had learned how to blend in, how to survive. I was a chameleon, and prison was just another environment that required adaptation.

The moment those heavy steel doors slammed shut behind me, sealing me inside, I felt it, a strange sense of calm. This wasn't juvie, this wasn't county jail; this was prison. The real deal. But I wasn't scared. Fear had been beaten out of me years ago. What I felt instead was a strange kind of ease, like I had finally landed somewhere I didn't have to pretend anymore. Out there, I was running from my past, from people who let me down, from people I let down. In here? None of that mattered. I wasn't Natasha the runaway, Natasha the disappointment, Natasha the screw-up. I was just another inmate, and for once, I belonged, and in here I would go by Montana, the cold-hearted bad bitch who had everything to gain and nothing to lose.

Prison was its own world, with its own rules, and I adapted fast. By the end of my first week, I had already figured out who ran the unit, which officers were dirty, who could get you what, and who to stay the fuck away from. Women like me, women who knew how to talk, how to listen, how to handle themselves, didn't have to fight their way in. We got embraced. And that's exactly what happened.

I made friends, real ones, or at least as real as prison friendships got. These weren't backstabbing like the ones on the outside. There was loyalty here, a kind of sisterhood built on the fact that we were all stuck in the same place, living the same life. Within a month, I had a solid prison family, women who looked out for each other, shared commissary when times were tight and made sure to make the best out of our time together.

And honestly, I was enjoying it.

Prison wasn't what people thought. Yeah, it was locked doors and concrete, but it was also life, a life most people would never understand. There were ways to make it enjoyable if you knew what you were doing. We had everything we needed. Makeup, if you had the money, you had access to it. If not, I learned early how to mix colored pencils with Vaseline to make lipstick, and eyeliner came from crushed-up pencil lead. If you wanted to perm or straighten your hair? Commissary had those for sale, you could purchase them and go to the beauty salon on the compound once a week. Cigarettes? There was always a way to get cigarettes. You could damn near get your hands on anything in there if you knew the right people.

The food was garbage, of course, so I never visited the chow hall. But that didn't matter. The real food came from us. We cooked items from the commissary menu in our dorm units and had meals together throughout the day. Ramen noodles, chips, packaged tuna, and some stolen seasoning packets? That was a five-star meal in there. We cooked in microwaves, since they had two in every dorm. Some girls could make cheesecakes out of graham crackers and coffee creamer. The creativity was insane.

And then there was the yard.

The rec yard was an actual rec yard; one of the biggest I'd ever seen. It was surrounded by tall fences topped with razor wire, and armed guards patrolled the perimeter, just in case anyone was dumb enough to try and run. But nobody did. What was the point? We weren't in county anymore; we were settled here. This wasn't a place you escaped from. This was a place you survived in.

The yard was where you really saw the social structure of the prison. The walkers, women who just did laps around the track, lost in their own thoughts or listening to music. The athletes, women who actually worked out, doing push-ups and running sprints like they had a tournament coming up. The groups, the ones who sat together in the same spots every day, running their own little circles of influence. And then there were the fighters, the ones who settled beef in the blind spots where the guards couldn't see.

I moved between groups easily, a chameleon as always. Some days I walked laps. Some days I played spades in the sun with a few women who had been locked up for decades, longer than I'd even been alive. Other days, I just sat on the benches, soaking in the heat, watching the world of prison unfold like a movie.

And the craziest part? I didn't miss the outside.

I didn't get letters. No calls. No visits. But that was fine. Nobody was waiting for me out there. The world outside had forgotten me, and honestly? I had forgotten it, too. I didn't sit around wondering what could've been, didn't waste time on regrets. That life was done. This was my life now, and I was making the best of it.

Somewhere deep down, I knew I should have been remorseful. I should have been thinking about my future, about making things right, about getting out and turning my life around. But the truth? I wasn't ready for that. Not yet.

I had spent my entire life feeling out of place, feeling like I didn't belong anywhere. But here? Here, I had a role. I had respect. I had power. For the first time in my life, I wasn't an outsider, I was somebody.

And so, at a time when I should have been scared, when I should have been apologizing, when I should have been planning for the life beyond these walls, I wasn't doing any of that. I was living. I had adapted, just like I always did. And I was having the time of my life.

Chapter 10: The Game

My bunkie, Sam, had been locked up for twelve years. She had settled into prison life so deeply that our cell wasn't just a space, it was her home. And like any woman who'd been down that long, she carried herself with a certain authority. She had routines and unspoken rules about how things went inside her space. I respected it. After all, I was new to this world, and Sam? Sam was surviving.

I had my own kind of survival skills though.

I wasn't just another girl lost in the system. I was pretty, and that mattered in here. Petite frame, long legs, high yellow skin with chinky eyes, I stood out, and I knew it. When I walked the yard, I felt the eyes on me, tracing every step. Some women watched with curiosity, others with jealousy, and some with something deeper, something dangerous. But it wasn't just the inmates who noticed me. The officers did too.

Prison was like kindergarten in a lot of ways. The rules were ridiculous. Stay inside the yellow lines. No talking in the halls. Shirts tucked in at all times. It was all just a power trip, designed to remind us we were nothing. But I had already learned that rules only mattered when you weren't the one bending them. And in a place like this, bending them was the only way to become the predator and not the prey.

I had heard the whispers about contraband, about who was sleeping with who, and which officers could be flipped with the right amount of charm. If you were pretty enough, smart enough, and played your hand just right, you could have it all. And I knew how to play, so I sat back and continued to observe.

I didn't care about the gossip until the night opportunity knocked, literally.

I was halfway asleep when I caught the thick, bitter scent of cigarette smoke. My nose wrinkled in disgust. I wasn't a smoker and hated that shit. I rolled over, eyes heavy, and that's when I saw him.

Sergeant Johnson.

The finest nigga on the compound. Built like a masterpiece. He was fine as hell. Stood about 6'4" with smooth dark skin like God took his time. Chestnut eyes that made you forget what you were talking about. Bow legged just enough to give him that slow, cocky walk. The kind that made you look twice, then one more time just to be sure. He didn't have to say a word. The way he moved said it all. Swagger loud as hell without making a sound. One of them ones you feel before he even steps in the room.

He didn't speak. Just took a puff from his cigarette and let the smoke roll from his lips slow, like he had all night.

I knew that look. It was hunger. That kind of look men give when they want to devour you but know they shouldn't.

Sam stirred in her bunk. She knew too. Johnson flicked the cigarette to the ground, stomped it out, and disappeared without a word.

The next morning, Sam didn't waste time.

"You need to use that shit, Montana," she said, lacing up her boots.

"For what? A honey bun and some eyeliner?" I scoffed.

She smirked. "That's because they don't know the game. Do less. Get more."

That was my kind of language.

It didn't take long for the game to start.

Every few nights, Sergeant Johnson would find an excuse to swing by. He'd catch a shift change, slide into the control room, and wait for me. And I'd show up. That tight little booth became our place.

Sometimes I'd straddle him, slow and intentional. I'd grind on him until I felt that bulge pressed between my thighs. My lips would brush his neck, and I'd circle my tongue around his earlobe, whispering my contraband requests like he was Santa at Christmas time. I never gave him sex. Just pressure. Just the feeling that it could happen. If he played it right.

Other times, I didn't even touch him. I'd stand there, lean in close, and just talk. Tell him how good he looked, how bad I wanted him, how horny he made me. And he would listen, breathing heavy, hand slipping down into his pants. I'd watch him stroke himself, slow at first, then faster, his eyes glued to my mouth while I talked him through it. I'd lick my lips on purpose, whispering how good he made me feel, how much he deserved it. I would squeeze my breast with my right hand and slide my left hand in my blues and start to flick my clitoris back and forth with my fingers. His moans would echo low in that room, and when he finished, I'd clean my hands like nothing happened and walk right out.

And when I had that fire building up in me from all that teasing, I knew where to go.

I'd slip into the showers and wait for Jade.

She knew what time it was. I didn't have to say much. I'd press my body against hers, warm and slick under the water, and she'd drop to her knees without hesitation. Her mouth worked like magic, slow and focused, tongue moving across every inch of me like she wanted to taste my soul. I'd moan soft, fingers tangled in her curls, letting her pull every bit of tension from my body. Every drop of heat Sergeant Johnson stirred in me got released between Jade's lips.

Jade was my girlfriend. I gave her affection. I gave her loyalty. She gave me peace and a release. And she never asked for more than I was willing to give.

I had it all. Makeup. Cigarettes. Extra canteen. Respect. A man in power wrapped around my finger and a woman with soft hands who knew how to release the freak in me when the doors closed.

The rest of them were giving up everything, for scraps. Begging for favors. Selling themselves short. I was running shit.

I wasn't praying for forgiveness or dreaming about release.

I was eating good and sleeping better. I was actually living like I had never lived before.

In prison, at that.

Chapter 11: The Set-Up

For ninety days, I ran shit on the compound. Life on the inside was sweet. I had canteen for days, connections with officers, and a bad bitch equivalent to myself to walk the compound with. I was untouchable, or so I thought. Then, the hate started. Nothing I wasn't used to; people had hated me my entire life just for knowing how to turn nothing into something. But prison hate? That was different. That shit was dangerous.

It started with the dry snitching. Whispers in the air about who had what, who was moving what, who was getting favors from the COs, correctional officers. It was never direct, just side comments, fake-ass conversations spoken just loud enough for the female officers to overhear.

Then came the cell searches. Twice a week, those same female officers, bitter faced, hard hair women who got off on making our lives miserable, would tear my cell apart. Dumping my property, flipping my mattress, going through my canteen like I wasn't the one who earned that shit. Every time they came, they left my space looking like a damn tornado had hit it. But I never let them see me sweat. I'd sit back, arms crossed, rolling my eyes, letting them do what they needed to do. Because I already knew. They wouldn't find shit. I wasn't stupid. I kept my contraband in places they'd never think to check.

But the hate wasn't just coming from the officers. It was coming from inside the compound too. I started hearing whispers about a girl named Slice. Her real name was Alice, but nobody called her that. She was known for cutting females with a straight razor, earning her nickname the hard way. She'd been locked up for years, and she had respect in here, the kind of respect that didn't come easy. And according to the tea on the compound? She wanted me gone.

Why? Because I was doing what she could never do. I didn't have to fight for my spot, I walked into it and took what I wanted. I didn't have to chase after the officers, they came to me. And that? That pissed her off, she had that type of envy and hatred that she couldn't mask.

I had been through too much in my life not to recognize the signs. From group homes to juvie, from detention centers to the streets, I knew when a setup was coming. And that day in the yard? I saw it before it even happened. We were headed out for rec time, walking in our straight prison line, shirts tucked in, no talking, just following the damn yellow path like good lil' inmates.

But I peeped her. Slice was posted in the cut, off to the side like she was waiting on something. Or someone. She was waiting on me. She had that same look I'd seen a hundred times before, the look of someone about to make a move and she had me fucked up.

I didn't wait for her to try it. I swung first. I caught her off guard, my fist connecting with her jaw before she even had the chance to react.

CLACK. Something hit the ground, her razor. She had been holding it on her tongue, tucked like a candy she planned to unwrap at the right moment. But my hit knocked it loose, sent it clattering onto the pavement before she could even grip it.

I didn't give her a chance to recover. I beat her ass. She swung, but I was faster. I grabbed her hair, yanked her forward, and dropped her with a hook to the ribs. When she stumbled, I straddled her, pounding her in the face and head. I wasn't new to this. I made sure she felt every damn hit.

By the time I was done, Slice wasn't Slice anymore. She was just Alice, the girl who got her ass beat. And the best part? The officers never even saw it. The fight happened so fast that by the time anybody turned their heads, I was already walking off like nothing happened. Like I hadn't just whipped someone's ass and went on about my day.

I thought that was the end of it. I thought Slice would take her loss and keep it pushing. But she wasn't built like that. Instead of holding the L, she took her snitch ass straight to the Captain's office. But she didn't tell them I whooped her ass. No. She did something worse. She told them about my alleged relationship with Sergeant Johnson. She threw my whole hustle into the light and me under the bus. And just like that, I was locked in confinement, pending investigation.

Chapter 12: The Hole

45 days. No canteen. No rec. No girlfriend. No nothing. Just four walls, a slab of metal they called a bed, and my own thoughts, the one thing I couldn't escape from. Confinement wasn't like prison. It was worse, and I was here pending investigation.

The cell was tiny, barely enough space to stretch out without touching cold concrete. No windows. The only view I had was the small metal slot in the door where they slid my trays through. Three times a day, the same cold food, the same lack of seasoning, the same reminder that I wasn't in control anymore. Showers? Once a week. I'd stand in line, shackled like an animal, waiting for my turn under lukewarm water that barely lasted long enough to wash the filth off my body. No privacy. Just steel and silence. No officers talked to us unless it was to bark orders. No one gave a damn if we were losing our minds in here. And the worst part? The silence.

At first, it felt suffocating, like a weight pressing on my chest, making me itch for movement, for conversation, for something. But silence doesn't exist in prison. Not really. Not when you have the vents.

The vents were our lifeline, our cellphones, our gossip lines, our news station, our therapy sessions. Inmates in confinement didn't have direct access to each other, but those vents… they carried voices.

That's how I found out Sarge tried to come see me. One night, I was lying on my back, staring at the cracked ceiling, when the vents came alive.

"Yo, why the hell Johnson in here? He never be in confinement."

"I'm telling you; that's her snack. That's why she locked up now."

"He trying to check on his lil' piece, but they on his ass now."

I didn't move. I didn't say a word. I just listened.

They were right, he had never been in confinement before. But the second he showed his face in here? It was over. The female officers had already been on my ass. Now, with his visit, they had proof that there was something there. That night, I laid on my bunk and knew one thing for sure: I wasn't making it back to my old dorm.

They made sure of that. When they moved me into confinement, they tossed everything. All my canteen, gone. No explanation, no warning. Snacks, supplies, hygiene, shit I worked hard to get, all of it in the trash. They ripped down my photos too, the little pieces of memory I had taped up on the inside of my locker. Pictures of Marcus, old Polaroids from years ago, even a letter I kept from my grandma. Shredded. Like none of it meant anything.

And the write-ups? Petty as hell. They hit me with a DR for having my uniform altered. One of the girls from laundry had tailored it to fit my petite shape, nothing drastic, just something that hugged my waist and made my ass stick out a little more. They called it "unauthorized modification of state property." Really, they were just mad I looked good in my blues, and they didn't.

They were trying to break me down. Strip me of everything I had built inside. The status, the comfort, the little bit of control I held onto. They wanted me invisible, silent, and forgotten. And for a second, I almost was. But I held it together. I stayed sharp. I stayed listening. Because even in that little box, even surrounded by cold walls and colder silence, I knew this wasn't the end. They could take my things, take my comfort, even take my name off the dorm roster… but they couldn't take me.

So, when the night came and that cell door buzzed open, I already knew what it meant.

Chapter 13: New Territory

The ride from Miami to Ocala was long as hell. I went from palm trees and sunshine to the cold-ass country, where the air smelled like cows and horse shit. I wasn't one to race bait, but from the moment I stepped off that bus, I could feel the racism all over this place.

The yard was hell, straight hills. Imagine being on a treadmill with the incline jumping from 1 to 10 over and over again as you walked. That was the daily workout, whether you wanted it or not. No flat ground. No mercy. Just walking at an angle all damn day. This is also where they held the inmates on death row, so the compound had a gloomy feeling wavering over it.

The intake process was one of the worst I had ever experienced. Imagine being butt-ass naked, standing in a shower, repeatedly being screamed at by three fat underpaid correctional officers who acted like they needed some dick in their lives. "Squat, cough, squat, cough." Damn, I thought to myself. How many times do they want to look at my insides before realizing that I don't have any contraband on me?

My transfer papers must've said a whole lot of something because they weren't letting me step foot on that compound without a proper cavity search. The compound was overcrowded and inmates needed to be either moved around or shipped off. I was shipped to an overpopulated prison, and they didn't even have a bed for me. I was housed in a confinement cell until things changed. The only difference was, I received yard time with the rest of the compound.

As soon as I stepped foot on the yard, I heard a familiar voice.

"Ayyyeee, I know that walk!"

I turned my head and there she was. Keisha. What the hell did she do that landed her here? Turns out, she was later on arrested for the run out and took a plea deal to escape the charges as well. Keisha knew I was a real bitch. Keisha could vouch for me here at Lowell.

Just like that, I wasn't alone anymore.

Word spread quick that I was transferred for an alleged officer relationship, and within a day, my name was ringing bells again. But I wasn't dumb. I kept my eyes open, watching who had the power and who was getting played. And what I saw? I wanted no parts of it.

The white girls had it on lock. They weren't running the yard because they were gangsta or pretty. Nah, they were actually having sex with the officers to receive their items. Cellphones, makeup, even heroin. I was now surrounded by a bunch of junkies, addicts. I wasn't about to play that game again. Instead, I did what I do best. I fell back and peeped the scene.

It didn't take me long to find Diamond. She was clean as hell, boots shiny, uniform pressed, waves spinning like a damn whirlpool. She carried herself with a masculine energy and besides the lil bee stings she had as breasts, she looked just like a man. She moved different from the rest of them, kept to herself, but had respect.

I ain't know much about her at first, but I knew one thing for sure. I wanted her.

Only problem? She had a girl. Some chick named Tina, who was locked up for murder.

At first, that sounded like a big deal, until I found out what really happened. Tina was a crackhead prostitute who killed her trick over twenty dollars. Sis wasn't a killer. She was a junkie who made a mistake. So, I played the back. Smiling at Diamond when she walked past, making sure she noticed me, but never pressing her. I waited. I learned everything I needed to know. Diamond had been down a few times, long enough to have outside people sliding money to the guards to keep her living good. She was top dawg on the yard, and I needed that kind of security.

And then, one day, it happened.

I was sitting in the dayroom, minding my business, when someone tapped my shoulder. I turned around. A note was slipped into my hand.

A kite.

I opened it up and smirked.

"Meet me by the laundry room after chow."

Just like that, I had taken someone's bitch.

Chapter 14: The Switch Up

Taking Diamond from Tina was too easy. I had been locked up long enough to know that women in prison were just like men in the free world. If you made them feel something, they were yours, and I had Diamond exactly where I wanted her. She started doing what they all do when they're into you, bringing me cigarettes to sell in my dorm, sliding me commissary, making sure I never wanted for shit. Just like that, I was good. No more waiting in long-ass lines at canteen, no more trading favors just to get what I needed. Diamond had outside money, and that meant I had outside money.

Diamond had been plotting for days, eyes cutting through the dorm like she already knew how it was gonna go down. She waited 'til third shift, when the guards got lazy and the cameras ain't catch every angle. That night, she slid me a note under my tray. Just a time. A place.

The canteen store.

When I stepped in, it was like a small pantry with an air conditioner unit inside. She locked the door and placed a key on the cashiers counter. She told me she gave the canteen worker a carton of cigarettes to rent us her store, so we didn't have to worry about being caught.

Diamond leaned against the counter, hoodie halfway zipped, eyes locked on me like I was the only thing in the room worth looking at. "You sure?" she asked, voice low and husky. I didn't answer. I didn't have to. She already knew.

She came over slowly. Her hands touched my waist, firm but gentle. Then her mouth followed. She kissed me like she had time to waste, like we weren't in the middle of a concrete cage. She didn't rush, didn't fumble. She took her time like this was sacred.

And when her head went down, she made every second feel like a confession. Soft at first. Then deep. Then still. She didn't stop until I forgot where I was, who I was and was begging her to stop.

Afterward, she stood up, licking her lips like she wasn't done. "You trust me?" she asked, pulling a glove from her pocket. I nodded, breath shaky.

She reached into a stash under the shelf and came back with a toothbrush, some folded pads, and a ripped-up t-shirt strip. I knew exactly what she was doing. Watched her wrap it tight, layer by layer, until it looked like something straight out a survival manual. Prison love in its rawest form.

When she was done, she looked at me and smirked. "Let me show you what else I know."

Diamond strapped that homemade dildo to her using a bra and a t-shirt, picked me up by my waist and slowly entered me while grinding slowly. By the time we were done, Diamond was drenched in sweat saying how she loved me the moment she saw me.

Damn, just like that? I thought to myself.

I wasn't about to fall for her though. Love didn't exist in prison. Power did. And I was about to make sure I had all of it. Now that I had a solid plug, I started flipping shit. Canteen? I resold it at double the price to girls who only got money once a month when the store was running low on items. Cigarettes? Easy money. A pack of Newports went for a hundred dollars' worth of canteen inside. Makeup, like mascara, lipstick, even perfume, all smuggled in, all sold to the highest paying inmate. I moved smart, kept my circle tight, my business low, and my hands clean. But power attracts enemies, and I had begun to gain too much too fast.

One night, I was on my bunk reading a book after count when I heard my name in the vents. "Yo, Montana need to watch her back. They talking about her in E-dorm." E-dorm was where all the bitter hoes stayed, the ones who wanted my spot but didn't have the hustle to take it. I sat up. "Who talking?" I asked through the vent. There was a pause. Then the response came back clear as day. "Tina."

I should've expected it. I had taken her bitch, taken her position, and now she wanted to run her mouth about me to whoever would listen. The old me would've handled it myself, but I didn't have to anymore. Because I had Keisha. At first, I had my doubts about Keisha, but behind these gates she had proven she was solid. She wasn't just my home girl, she was my muscle. I didn't even have to ask twice. She lived for this type of shit.

We were all sittin' at rec, Keisha lacing up them dusty black boots like she was suiting up for a damn stage play. Real calm, real focused, like she already knew how this act was gonna end. She looked up at me, eyes sharp. "So what's the move? You want her touched or embarrassed?" I leaned back, smirked like the villain I ain't deny being. "Embarrassed. I want the whole compound to know she soft." Keisha cracked a grin. "Say less."

Next morning at breakfast felt like opening night. Lights. Camera. Chaos. Tina over there posted with her lil bootleg cheer squad, cackling loud, flipping her braids like she just knew she was untouchable. Sis was mid-joke when Keisha strutted in like she owned the whole damn chow hall.

Didn't even blink. Didn't even grab a tray. She walked right up to Tina, snatched hers like it was a prop, and dumped the whole plate; grits, eggs, mystery meat, straight in her lap. The whole table gasped like someone hit rewind on the scene.

Tina jumped up, eyes bugged, face twisted like she smelled herself. But before she could pop off, Keisha leaned in real close, like she was about to whisper a prayer. "Keep Montana's name out ya raggedy ass mouth. Next time, it won't be food on your lap. It'll be a stretcher."

Silence. Tina froze. All that mouth? Gone. Sis looked like a toddler that just got scolded in front of the class. Hands shaking. Pride leaking. Soul leaving the building. She didn't say not one word. Just sat there, soaked in shame, marinating in that hot plate of karma.

Keisha slid back over to me like she just wrapped a scene on a daytime drama. Cool. Collected. Not a crumb on her. "Handled."

And that was it. Tina learned the hard way. From that day forward, my name stayed real safe in everybody's mouth

Chapter 15: The Chapel Hustle

Lowell wasn't as bad as I had initially thought. Once I figured out the system, I realized we had more freedom here than anywhere else I had been locked up.

And with Diamond? I was living good.

She had pull, and just like that, she had me moved into her dorm. Now, instead of being in a large room with over 50 bunks out in the open, I was laid up with my girl, stretched out in that tiny-ass bunk, pretending it was a king-sized bed.

The officers? Chill, for the most part.

Yeah, they did their rounds and screamed orders, when necessary, but if you stayed in your lane, they left you alone. Some of them were dirty, some of them were just tired, and some of them didn't care at all, as long as you didn't make their job harder than it had to be.

But Sundays?

Sundays were a whole different world.

Every Sunday morning, the officers would open up the chapel and let inmates go watch movies.

That was supposed to be the Lord's house, a place to get your spirit right, a moment of peace from all the chaos in here.

But these hoes?

They were in there getting their coochie's played in.

In the Lord's house!

The nerve.

I ain't judge, though. I just sat back, looking pretty, minding my own business, while Diamond ran her Sunday hustle.

Diamond had been locked up long enough to know the money game inside and out.

And on Sundays? Sundays was when Diamond really filled up our lockers.

She would get the cheapest cigarettes smuggled in and break them down, re-rolled them into smaller pieces, and sold them for quadruple the price. The inmates never asked what the brand was, then never complained, just paid and went on about their day.

It was genius.

One cigarette could turn into four sales. And since tobacco was like gold in prison, people paid whatever she charged.

She'd be posted up in the back of the chapel, fingers working quick, stuffing, rolling, sealing. And me? I'd just sit there, playing with my hair, watching her run her business like a CEO.

She wasn't just my girl. She was my partner. This went on for my entire stay at Lowell and soon my release was approaching.

Chapter 16: The Release

The last few days leading up to my release felt like time was playing tricks on me. One minute, it felt like I had all the time in the world left inside those walls. The next, it felt like the days were slipping through my fingers faster than I could hold on.

Diamond wasn't taking it well. She tried to act unbothered, but I could see it in her eyes. The way she'd pull me close at night, the way she kept looking at me like she was memorizing my face, like she didn't know if she'd ever see me again once I walked out those gates. But instead of sitting in our feelings, she did what she did best. She made sure I left like a legend.

The night before I was set to go, she threw me a full-blown going away party in the dorm. The officers working that night weren't tripping. They knew Diamond had pull, and as long as we kept the chaos contained, they weren't about to shut it down. And when I say party, I mean party.

She had the girls make space in the dayroom. Commissary snacks were passed around like we were at a real celebration. Somebody even made a speaker out of a radio and a couple of old wires, and next thing I knew, the whole dorm was vibing like we were at the club.

Then came the lap dances.

I was sitting back in one of the plastic chairs, laughing, sipping on some knockoff soda like it was a top-shelf drink, when Diamond clapped her hands and pointed at me. "Ayo, Montana gettin' one last show before she go!" The dorm lost it. Girls were hyping each other up, the energy in the room turning wild. One by one, they started giving each other lap dances like we weren't in the middle of a damn prison.

Then Diamond strutted over, pushing somebody out of the way. "Nah," she said, eyes locked on me. "If anybody givin' Montana a send-off, it's me." The whole dorm lost it. She pulled me to my feet and led me to the showers.

The head was immaculate.

That night, I laughed harder than I had in a long time. For a moment, I almost forgot where I was. Almost forgot that by morning, I'd be walking out of here for good. Almost.

I barely slept. By the time the sun started creeping through the tiny, fogged-up windows, I was already awake, staring at the ceiling. Diamond was curled up beside me, her breathing slow and steady, but I knew she wasn't really sleeping either. She just didn't wanna say it out loud.

When the officer finally called my name for release, the whole dorm got quiet for a second. Even the ones who weren't my people, even the ones who didn't really fuck with me like that, they all just kinda watched. Diamond sat up, rubbing her eyes like she was just waking up, but I knew better.

I grabbed my stuff, what little I had, and turned to her one last time. "You good?" I asked. She smirked, but her eyes said something else. "Always." I nodded, knowing damn well we were both lying. Then I walked out.

Walking through those last set of doors was surreal. I had spent so much time dreaming about this moment, but now that it was here, it didn't feel real. I didn't feel scared. I didn't feel excited. I just felt… ready. I had spent years behind that fence, watching, learning, listening. Prison didn't scare me. The streets didn't scare me. The only thing that ever scared me was being broke, and after everything I had soaked up in that place, that was never gonna happen again.

When I finally stepped outside, I blinked against the sunlight, feeling the warmth on my skin like it was the first time in forever. And then I saw her.

Alexis.

I stopped in my tracks. She was leaning against a Nissan Altima, arms crossed, watching me like she had all the time in the world. We hadn't spoken in years. Not before I got locked up, not when I was in the streets, and definitely not while I was inside. But here she was, waiting.

I walked up slow, keeping my face unreadable. "How the hell you know I was getting out?" She shrugged. "I heard. Looked you up. Figured you'd need a ride." I stared at her, trying to figure out her angle.

I could've pressed her, could've questioned why now, but honestly, I didn't care. She was here. That was enough.

I threw my bag in the backseat and climbed in, the door creaking as it shut behind me. Alexis slid into the driver's seat, turning the key. The engine rumbled to life, and just like that, I was gone.

Where to now, I thought.

Chapter 17: Out the Gate

When I got out, I stayed with Alexis for a few months until I could catch my breath and get my money up. Life after prison didn't wait for nobody, so I got straight to it. Worked at an ice cream shop during the day, then hit the strip club at night. I wasn't one of the pole-spinning, upside-down ballerinas. Nah. I was the one gliding through the crowd, slow grinding on laps, collecting dollars and phone numbers. I made eye contact, moved my hips just right, whispered in ears, and had the guys paying bills late to take care of me. Never a club near by though, always one at least an hour away with white women and plus sized hoes. I knew exactly what I was doing whenever I'd pick my new location to dance at.

First thing I bought was a car. A '97 Ford Contour. Burgundy, clean inside and out. It wasn't flashy, but it was mine. After the car, came my own spot. My name on the lease, my key, my peace. Me and Alexis stayed close. Even after I moved, we ran together. She was like my sister. We partied, hustled, and laughed about everything and nothing.

By now, my name was ringing in the streets. People knew me. Some talked shit, said I was always in jail, always chasing fast money. But I knew something they didn't. When people talk, other people get curious. Curiosity brought attention. Attention brought opportunity. Especially with men. Her man, her sister's man, whoever had the fattest wallet, that's who got my time. I wasn't loyal to anyone but myself.

Then came Quincy.

He wasn't cute. Let's be clear. He was short like a dwarf and had a big ass head. But Quincy was known for one thing. Money. Real money. He drove one of the most expensive cars in the city, and not one white tooth in his mouth. All gold teeth with a heavy gold chain to match.

We met on some hustling shit. He needed a driver. Someone who could ride quiet, stay solid, and get him where he needed to go without asking questions. That was me. I drove him across state lines, back roads, big cities. I watched him make tens of thousands of dollars, and every time he counted up, he handed me my 15% like clockwork. Fast money. No clock-ins. No bosses. I was hooked.

And slowly, he grew on me.

Money'll do that.

He flirted heavy. I played it cool. He'd say slick shit, try to grab my hand while I was driving, and I'd just smirk and pull away. But one night, we were at a hotel after a long run. He was pacing, stressed. His girl had been calling all night, back-to-back, blowing his line up. He looked tired, like he hadn't exhaled in weeks.

I told him, "Relax. I got you."

I ain't gon' lie. I put it on him. Every ounce of pressure he was feeling, I pulled it out of him with every stroke, every breath, every whisper in his ear. That night I went from his driver to his peace, his escape, his partner. After that, the money came faster. I didn't just drive. I helped count, weigh, organize. I was in the room for all the plays. He trusted me more than anybody.

Only thing is, he had a girl.

She wasn't some "as long as he comes home at night" broad either. She knew something was up. Quincy told her we were just doing business, but she wasn't buying that. Every time we were out making moves, she was calling, texting, threatening. "I know you with that bitch," she'd scream through the phone. He'd mute her, roll his eyes, and keep it pushing. Me? I wasn't worried. While she was crying at home, I was riding in the front seat, windows down, music up, nails done off his coins.

I was his calm in the chaos. Every night after a long day, I made sure he emptied every drop of stress before he went home. He'd lay there, eyes closed, breathing heavy, whispering he wished he could stay with me forever, some nights he did.

But I wasn't built to be owned.

I still had two dudes I kept in rotation from the club. Quincy was obsessed, but I wasn't giving up my freedom just because he was in his feelings. He had to fall in line just like the rest. He knew about them too. Couldn't say much though. He had a whole woman at home. The double standard was loud, but I didn't care. I was living good, living free.

His girl? She started showing up at places I'd be. She keyed my car once, left notes on my doorstep, even followed me into a store pretending to be on the phone. She wanted to scare me off, but I wasn't built like that. I had my own crib, my bills paid, my fridge full, all off her man. She wasn't about to ruin my good living.

Mama had no choice but to share.

I wasn't giving him up. Not when he was paying my rent, buying my clothes, and sucking me dry. If she wanted to cry and throw tantrums, she could do it from home. Me? I was too busy counting stacks and living unbothered. She should've thanked me, really. I gave her a break. Gave her man back fed, relaxed, and half asleep.

Chapter 18: All Gas, No Brakes

At 21, I was having my way. No rules. No ceilings. No responsibilities except staying free and stacking paper. I had my own apartment, a luxury whip that hummed smooth, and a passport full of fake names. I was flying state to state like I was somebody important. But what I was really doing was running it the fuck up.

Quincy had put me on to scamming, and once I got a taste, I was hooked. It was better than the strip club, better than boosting, better than anything I'd ever done. I was already used to the rush. I'd been chasing danger since I was a teen, so this? This was just the next level. High-stakes. High-reward. It was thrilling. Illegal, yeah. But thrilling? Even more.

Driving for Q turned into something way more lucrative. I leveled up from passenger to player. The check game. That's where the real money lived. Q had the stolen IDs, the fake names, the bogus checks, and the accounts already wired up. All he needed was somebody to walk into the bank and play the role. That's where I came in.

Prison had taught me a lot more than how to survive. It taught me how to do my makeup, how to transform. So, when it came time to make myself look like some woman named "Rhonda Williams" or "Christina M. Daniels," I knew exactly how to blend, bake, and beat my face into a new identity.

I'd sit in the car, engine running, going over the name on the ID out loud like I was rehearsing for a play. "Christina… M… Daniels," I'd say in the mirror. Practicing the signature. Memorizing the birthday. Matching the smile. Then I'd step out like I belonged there, heels clicking, bag swinging, nerves locked tight behind lip gloss and fake confidence.

And the whole time, Q would be laid out in the backseat, phone in hand, guiding me through every move.

"Tell 'em your address if they ask. It's on the ID."

"If they take the check to the back, run!"

"If shit feel off at any time, leave."

And I followed every word. Cool under pressure. Smooth in the lobby. I'd walk in and smile like the check was just another errand in my day. And when the teller gave me that nod, handed me the receipt, I'd strut out like I'd just made rent money the clean way. Get in the car. Look at Q. Grin. We'd be gone before they even finished logging the transaction.

But not every ID matched my face. And Q wasn't the type to waste anything.

So, when I didn't fit the picture, we'd do something bold. We'd find a crackhead.

Yup. A real-life, off-the-street, high-as-a-kite crackhead. Q would pull up in a rough part of town in whatever state we were in, roll the window down, and say, "Hey baby, tryna make some money real quick?"

They'd hop in without asking questions. Didn't care where we were going or what it was about. We'd take them to a motel, let them shower, feed them, dress them in some cheap heels and a basic wig. I'd do their makeup myself, try to make them look like the woman on the ID. Practice lines with them. Coach them on what to say, how to stand, how to sign the name like it was theirs.

Some of them would fumble it. Too shaky, too twitchy, too damn high. But every now and then, one of them would pull it off, and we'd split the hit. Q always made sure they got their cut. Enough to disappear with for a few days and stay out our way. Then we'd be off to the next city, the next name, the next bag.

And when the ID did match me? That's when it was lights, camera, action.

We hit bank after bank. Flew across the country. Every stop was a new opportunity. I didn't just play the role. I became her. Sweet but confident. Soft but firm. The kind of woman who looked like she had a mortgage and a husband in real estate. I was everybody and nobody, all at once.

And after every successful run, we celebrated. Sometimes with steak and champagne. Sometimes with sex in the backseat right there in the parking lot. Me still in character, telling him to call me by the name on the I.D. Him grabbing my face like I was gold. Breathing hard. Whispering, "You raw as fuck."

I was.

Every check that cleared, every account we drained, every teller that smiled at me not knowing I was robbing them blind. That was power. That was real confidence. I wasn't punching no clock. I was punching into a new tax bracket.

I had money in my bag. Keys to a car I didn't finance. Receipts from malls all over the country. I didn't feel bad. Not when I was living good. Not when I was free. Not when I was draped in labels with a man who adored me and feared me at the same time.

I knew it wouldn't last forever. We were running wild. Too flashy. Too loud. But at 21? I didn't care about the end. I was just riding the high.

And baby, I was sky fucking high.

Chapter 19: Crash Season

By 21, I had the city on lock. I wasn't just known, I was respected. Talked about. Watched. Feared a little too. I was that girl. A known female hustler. Pretty face, slick mouth, always on go. People remembered me from back in the day, from the wild-ass house parties me and Nasir used to throw. So it only made sense to jump back into that scene. Only this time, I was getting paid to pop out.

I started teaming up with the local club promoters, hosting parties, showing face, turning regular-ass nights into events. The life of the party.

Me and Q had gotten closer over time. And after a year, I was in love. That nigga loved me too. He still had his girl, but he had me too. I was cool with that. She was the one with the problem.

And baby, she was a big one.

Now I'm tall, but I'm petite. This girl had thick legs, thick arms, thick feet. She was solid. So every time she wanted to fight me, I ran. Yep, sure did. I know I've been through the system in all types of ways, but never have I ever encountered a woman her size. And to top it off, word around town was that she was known for beating bitches up. I wanted no parts.

And truthfully, I didn't even know why she wanted to fight me when me and her weren't the only ones he was in a relationship with. That man had money, so he had plenty of bitches. Hell, she and I could've had him together at that time and I wouldn't have cared. She was pretty, a little thicker, but fuckable if it ever had to come down to it. Anything to keep my coins coming in.

This girl and I were at war. Literally.

Anytime I stepped outside, drama.

And I loved outside.

One day, I made her, and her friends meet me at the park, thinking I was finally going to fight her. Once everyone arrived at the park, I rode by blasting music with my windows down, laughing and talking shit. I wasn't getting out. I just wanted to piss her off.

The next time that girl caught me, she beat my ass. I tried to run, but she caught me. Right outside the club. In front of everybody.

I'm walking out with my high heels on, a fresh sew-in wrap in my head, makeup done, about to give valet my key to bring my truck around, and who do I see? Miss Thang with her wrestling boots on and bikini bottoms. Yes, in the club. Walking toward me.

This is when I tried to run.

Next thing you know, Wonder Woman snatched me from behind and started knocking me in my head. She must've hit me a little too hard, because once I got to my vehicle and realized my tracks that were sewn in were hanging and my face was scratched up, I drove straight to her grandma's house, where she was living at, and burst out the front window.

That'll teach her.

She never touched me again. But she definitely hated me for life.

After all of that, oh Q ass was finna pay for that.

Every time you turned around, I needed something. I had also been seen with dudes that weren't him out in public, and that crushed him. But I needed to get him a little deeper, and that's when it hit me. Fake a pregnancy.

So I did. Got him for a couple thousand dollars and hollered abortion.

I would still hit him up from time to time but nothing too serious. I even stopped going out of town with him. I had moved on. I saw who I wanted, when I wanted. If I loved them one day, I could hate them the next. That's how I liked it.

Q had me falling and I didn't even realize I was allowing yet another sorry ass nigga to make a fool out of me for a dollar. It was hard to shake Q at first, because no matter who I dealt with, he was willing to play his position and not speak to me in public. He had his situations, and I had mine. So I dealt my own cards, and I was the queen.

To make my own fast and easy money, I started boosting and selling clothes to everyone in the city. I stole it all—from house supplies to party orders. Baby clothes to plus sized men. Costumes on Halloween and toys on Christmas. The money was quick and easy, and I didn't need anyone for anything.

I had stolen things in my past before, but not like this. I was a full-time thief. Out the house by 8am and in no later than 6pm. Shoplifting from Coral Gables to West Palm Beach on a daily basis. Fulfilling orders was my thing, and I didn't take on any new customers unless they spent $100 or better.

I kept my money in cash. Always. I didn't trust nobody. I had a shoebox full of it, stuffed and hidden between other boxes in my closet just in case anyone ever broke into my apartment. I made sure I never had to depend on a soul.

Q?

Q who???

I forgot he even existed.

By now I was deep into my new lifestyle, too deep.

Shoplifting. Partying. Thuggin, literally. That crash and burn lifestyle I always seemed to fall into was back again, and this time, I wasn't even trying to escape it. I dove headfirst like I needed the chaos to breathe.

I'd hit stores during the day, load up on whatever I could get out with, then hit the streets at night like life was sweet. I was getting money fast and spending it even faster. One day I'd be at Walmart walking out with carts full of stolen shit, the next I'm in the VIP section like I was born rich. New hair, new fit, fresh beat on my face, drink in one hand, phone in the other, recording every moment like it wouldn't all come crashing down.

The adrenaline from stealing was better than sex. Walking in calm, eyes focused, walking out with bags and not paying a damn thing. I didn't care about the risk. I didn't even flinch. Half the time I knew they were watching me and still dared them to say something. They didn't. I'd get back in my car, go home and prepare to sell the items I'd just gotten.

Then it was off to the club. I didn't miss a night. If the city was jumping, I was right there in the mix. Throwing ass, catching drinks, living my life. Nobody knew I had just hit three different malls that same day. I moved smooth. I looked good. I talked slick. People saw the outside, but inside I was on fire, and not the good kind. I was spinning.

Truth is, I had been to jail and out more times than I could even count. I never stressed it too much. I either had enough cash to bond myself out, or some dude I was messing with at the time would come through and take care of it. It became normal. Too normal. I'd be gone for a few days, come right back out like nothing ever happened. Change my wig, get back to the hustle, and keep it pushing.

But that last time? Something hit different.

I did a nine-month bid in county. They put me in the Christian unit. That meant church all day, every day. And yeah, I was still me. Still cracking jokes with anybody I caught a positive vibe from and staying out of everyone else's faces who seemed weird or made me feel uneasy. But something started shifting.

I started thinking about that funny feeling I always got when something wasn't right. That gut feeling that told me when to leave, when to fall back, when to cut somebody off. I used to ignore it, brush it off like it was nerves. But being in that cell, having nothing but time to sit with myself, I realized that was discernment. That was God trying to talk to me.

And for once, I was listening.

I didn't turn into a saint overnight, but I started understanding myself on a deeper level. I started asking questions. Started praying more. Started reading scripture just to pass time, but the words started speaking to me. I wasn't just existing anymore. I was reflecting. For the first time, I wasn't running. I was facing everything I kept stuffing under the surface. All the trauma. All the pain. All the habits I had built to survive.

Something in me cracked open.

I wasn't just a hustler or a pretty face or the wild girl who always kept a bag. I was a woman with purpose, with power, with calling. I started feeling like maybe everything I had been through was leading me somewhere. Maybe I wasn't just crashing for no reason. Maybe the wreckage had meaning.

That jail cell became the first place I started healing.

Slow. Quiet. But real.

Chapter 20: New Money, Same Me

When I got out, I told myself I was gonna do things a little different. Not too different. Just enough to get what I wanted without always looking over my shoulder. I still had that fire in me, still sharp, still slick, still drawn to money like I had a sixth sense for it. But this time, I wanted to see what it felt like to get money that didn't come with handcuffs.

I started working as a collection's rep for a loan company. Sit at a desk, clock in, make calls, collect payments. It was legit, but it didn't feel like a regular job to me. I was making good money. Real good. My hourly pay was solid, and the monthly percentages on top made me feel like I was finessing the system legally. The more I collected, the more I made. And I could talk my ass off, so it was nothing to me.

I'd come to work dressed like a CEO in training. Nails done, lashes on, slick edges, lip gloss poppin. I handled business. My call time stayed high; my collections hit goals. I wasn't one of them lazy girls watching the clock. I was chasing checks.

But even while I was sitting at that desk, I was still me. That little voice in me that used to whisper when something felt off was louder now. I didn't call it God. I just knew it was my discernment, and I finally started trusting it. If a vibe was off, I moved around. Quick. No convo. No closure. People came and went like city buses. If you didn't feel right, you didn't stay long. I had outgrown trying to force things that didn't feel aligned.

And people noticed it. I wasn't as available. I was selective about who I answered the phone for, who I let pull up, who got access to me. I wasn't wasting time or energy on nobody I wouldn't want in my corner if shit hit the fan.

One day at work, this man came in to make a payment. He was dressed clean, gold watch, cologne that hit before he even made it to the front desk. He tried to be smooth, asking questions he already knew the answers to just to talk longer. I played along. Gave him just enough to keep him curious. I knew what he was doing. He ended up leaving with my number and I let him think it was his idea.

By that weekend I was sitting in his Benz with the seat warmers on, eating seafood with a view of the city like I was living out a soft life commercial. He was giving luxury. And I ain't even have to fake a smile. He had money, charm, ambition. The whole package.

But of course, nothing is ever that perfect.

Two weeks later, I found out he had a whole wife in another state, two kids, and was running one of his businesses out of his mama's garage. I wasn't mad. I had been through worse. I didn't argue, didn't block him right away. I just slowly stopped responding. The last time he texted me; I left him on read while I was sitting in the breakroom drinking a free coffee with extra cream and smiling at my direct deposit.

I was finally in a season where I didn't need to blow up or crash out over nobody. I let karma do the heavy lifting.

Everything was smooth. The money was flowing, I had my own spot, my bills were paid before they were due, and I had options. If I wanted company, I had it. If I wanted space, I took it. I had finally learned how to be alone without being lonely. That was new for me.

But just when life starts feeling too good, something always comes to test you.

The test came in the form of an old lesson I thought I had already passed. A man.

This one came in like he was sent. Smooth. Grown. Quiet but focused. The type to study you before he speaks. He didn't come in fast, he moved like he had time. Played it cool. Said the right things, did just enough to feel safe. Brought me food, rubbed my feet, kissed my forehead like he meant it. He knew what to say. And for a minute, I believed him.

I let him in. Not just into my space, but into parts of me I had protected for years. I was still healing, still learning myself, but I gave him the front-row seat. And slowly, he started showing who he really was.

I asked a question and he got defensive. He started disappearing, always having some excuse. Then came the mood swings. The slick comments. The subtle disrespect. My gut told me something was off, and this time I didn't ignore it.

I confronted him.

And that's when he showed his true self.

He beat me.

Bad.

Knots on my face. A bloody lip. My eye damn near swollen shut. All because I asked him a question. And when it was over, he stood there like I had done something wrong. Started packing his shit like he was the victim.

And my dumb ass begged him to stay.

That became the cycle.

He'd beat me.

I'd cover the bruises with makeup.

Tell people I fell or bumped my face.

Lie about my happiness.

Pretend I was okay.

But inside, I was breaking.

The final time, I snapped.

He had been beating and beating me and I had enough.

Enough of lying. Enough of covering up. Enough of being scared in my own home.

I stabbed him.

Grabbed a steak knife from the drawer and stuck it in his side. Pepper sprayed him while he screamed. Pushed him outside on the porch and locked my door. My whole body was shaking but I didn't stop. I locked every door, every window, and I sat in the silence while he banged and screamed outside.

That was the last I ever saw of him.

But the damage was done.

I went into a deep depression.

It was like all the shit I had been carrying from my past finally caught up with me. Childhood trauma. Betrayal. Abuse. Feeling unworthy. Feeling unloved. I realized I had never healed from anything. I just kept running, kept surviving, kept pretending.

I stopped answering calls. Barely ate. Slept all day. Cried at night. My spirit was heavy. And instead of dealing with it, I numbed it.

That's when I started popping ecstasy.

One pill turned into two. One weekend turned into every weekend. I didn't want to feel anything. I didn't want to face nothing. I just wanted to float. To feel good for a few hours. To forget the pain. Forget the blood. Forget the way he used to choke me and say he loved me in the same breath.

But you can only run for so long.

And my high started to feel like a slow fall.

Chapter 21: The Wait

Everything caught up with me, again. After I stabbed him, after the pills, after the pretending, I went right back into survival mode. I didn't heal; I just hid. I went back to what I knew. Boosting. Lying. Running game. Anything to keep from sitting with myself. Anything to keep from feeling all that pain that was eating me alive from the inside out.

But the streets had changed. And I wasn't moving as smart as I thought I was.

I started getting arrested. Constantly. County to county. One week I was in Dade, next week Broward. Palm Beach. Orange County. I was being transported in chains, picked up for warrants in different cities. I couldn't keep up. My name was hot. My face was familiar. I'd walk into holding and girls would be like, "Damn, you again?" And I'd laugh it off, but deep down I was tired. My spirit was tired.

The worst part wasn't even the time. It was the treatment.

These jails were worse than anything I'd ever seen, even prison. Dirty, cold, nasty attitudes. The guards didn't care if you were sick, hungry, bleeding, nothing. They'd ignore you like you didn't exist. I saw women in those cells get raped by other women. Not once. Not twice. Regular. The screams still sit in the back of my mind. And the sickest part? It didn't even faze most of the guards. They turned the other way.

It was like being trapped in a dark, empty room. Some of those women were beyond help. Some were just broken in ways the world would never understand. And me? I was somewhere in between. I didn't belong there, but I did. I was out of control, and the system was finally closing in.

Eventually, I bonded out. Not once. Not twice. But three times. I was out on bond in three different counties, running back and forth to court, living in limbo. Every courtroom felt like a death sentence. The looks from the judges. The quiet whispers in the back of the courtroom. My name being called like I was just another case to push through the system.

Then came the hit.

One judge looked at my record and said enough is enough. He ruled that I be held with no bond until sentencing. Told me I was a flight risk. Told me I needed to sit. Told me I was dangerous.

And just like that, I was possibly heading back in the chain gang.

Only difference this time. I has a few men I dealt with on the outside who made sure I was straight. Money on my books. Packages. Phones. Whatever I needed, I had it. So if I did have to do time again, I was gonna do it with my feet up and my head high.

But that waiting period before sentencing? That was a mind game.

Every night I stared at the ceiling wondering what was next. Would they give me two years? Five? Ten? Would I walk? Was God gonna show up for me or was this the price I had to pay for all the chaos I caused? I didn't know.

I sat in that cold-ass cell with my back against the wall and my spirit quiet.

No tears.

No calls.

Just silence.

Because now, all I could do was wait.

And what happened next…

Well, you just gon' have to see.

AUTHOR'S NOTE

If you made it to the end of this book, thank you. For real. Thank you for taking the time to read my story, sit with my pain, witness my mess, and still make it through with me.

This wasn't easy to write. Reliving some of these moments broke me all over again. But I knew I had to get it out. I knew there was somebody somewhere who needed to hear it raw. No sugar-coating. No filters. Just truth.

I didn't write this for sympathy. I wrote it for the girl who's been through hell and still wakes up swinging. For the woman who's covering bruises with makeup, lying to her friends about being "okay," and forgetting who the hell she is. For anybody who's ever felt like giving up, like they weren't enough, like life was against them. I see you. I am you.

I've been to the bottom. I've made choices I'm not proud of. I've hurt people. I've been hurt. I've cried myself to sleep in jail cells, in trap houses, in hotel rooms, and in my own damn bed. But through all of that, I'm still here.

And that means something.

This book is proof that you can survive what was meant to destroy you. That even when the world counts you out, there's still a version of you that's worth fighting for. I'm not perfect. I'm not fixed. But I'm growing. I'm learning how to love myself out loud. I'm learning how to walk in truth and not shame. And I'm learning how to forgive the old me for not knowing better.

To everyone who supported me, pushed me, or even just believed in me from a distance—thank you. Your love held me together in ways I'll never be able to explain.

And to the younger me…

I'm so damn proud of you.

This isn't the end. This is just the part where I finally took control of the pen and started writing my own story.

With nothing but love and gratitude,

Cousin ;)

Made in the USA
Columbia, SC
15 April 2025